A Turning to God

Also by Cardinal Basil Hume OSB:

Basil in Blunderland
Footprints of the Northern Saints
The Mystery of the Cross
The Mystery of the Incarnation
The Mystery of Love

A Turning to God

Cardinal Basil Hume OSB

Edited by Patricia Hardcastle Kelly

DARTON · LONGMAN + TODD

First published in 2007 by
Darton, Longman and Todd Ltd
1 Spencer Court
140–142 Wandsworth High Street
London SW18 4JJ

Reprinted 2008 (twice)

ISBN-10   0-232-52701-6
ISBN-13   978-0-232-52701-8

A catalogue record for this book is available from the British Library.

Phototypeset by YHT Ltd, London
Printed and bound in Great Britain by
Athenaeum Press Limited, Gateshead, Tyne & Wear

Contents

❦

Foreword

The personal dedication of Cardinal Basil Hume to prayer was obvious to anyone who ever knew or met him. He carried about within himself a still centre that was almost tangible. It was, I think, the thing that most attracted people to him. Indeed, it was the source that most informed his character and gave him that wonderful simplicity and incisiveness when faced with matters of Church or State. I believe that it was the thing that most held him together during the many phases of his life and gave him the tranquillity to face every difficulty and crisis with equanimity.

He most certainly would not have readily recognised within himself this special quality that was so obvious to others. He would have been the first to say how important prayer was and how one needed to work at it, day in and day out, without expecting any sort of consolation. Indeed I recall how Cardinal Winning, during an informal gathering of bishops who were talking about prayer, asked Cardinal Hume how he as a former monk and now a bishop prayed. After a momentary awkwardness and a turning in his chair, came the reply, 'Oh, I'm such a flop'. We knew then as we know now how untrue that was. Whatever the estimation of his own efforts might have been it was clear that God had deeply touched this great yet humble priest.

He once noted that 'wisdom and understanding are the fruits of prayer. We become clearer about the end to which we are travelling on life's pilgrimage, and more certain of the means to be adopted to get there. And however rough the going becomes, we have the courage to go on, remaining deep down at peace.' He possessed, despite his perceived floppishness, an inner something that spoke of that peace and of his dedication to 'life's pilgrimage with God'.

This compilation by Patricia Hardcastle Kelly opens up for us something of the prayerful insights of Cardinal Hume. These insights were influenced by an ever-growing understanding of how God was continually drawing close to him and, indeed, everyone if only they gave time to notice. The springboard for these insights came from his love of sacred scripture which led him to ponder and led him to prayer. He once said, 'Trying to pray is prayer and it is very good prayer. The will to try is also [God's] gift.' This book is for all who wish to step out on that journey of discovery which, in turning to God, leads to a deeper understanding of how close God is to us and how only in him we, too, can find that still centre that brings with it a peace that permeates life.

✠ *Arthur Roche*
Bishop of Leeds

Editor's Note

The choice of scripture readings was guided by the common lectionary for Lent. I have offered a title and a short prayer for each daily reflection; otherwise, all the words are Cardinal Hume's own, taken from (largely unpublished) homilies and addresses.

The Trustees of Ampleforth Abbey and Cardinal Hume's literary executors have all kindly allowed me to use extracts from his homilies and talks as Abbot of Ampleforth (1963–76) and Cardinal Archbishop of Westminster (1976–99). This would, of course, have been impossible without the work of the archivists at Ampleforth Abbey, and, especially, of the late Heather Craufurd, who typed up, filed and numbered Cardinal Hume's homilies, talks and addresses over more than twenty years.

Anthea Craigmyle has very generously allowed me to use *Annunciation with Black Cat* for the cover image.

Bishop Arthur Roche has kindly agreed to write the Foreword, offering an insight into Cardinal Hume's approach to prayer and life beyond his public role as Archbishop of Westminster.

Brendan Walsh suggested this project to me and, despite all evidence to the contrary, continued to have confidence in my ability to submit a manuscript on time.

Cardinal Hume himself has, I am quite certain, been overseeing and guiding this work from a better place.

Scripture readings are taken from *The Jerusalem Bible* (Darton, Longman and Todd, 1966).

Patricia Hardcastle Kelly

Daily Readings for Lent

A time of grace
Ash Wednesday

❧

Scripture Reading

'But now, now – it is Yahweh who speaks – come back to me with all your heart, fasting, weeping, mourning.' Let your hearts be broken, not your garments torn, turn to Yahweh your God again, for he is all tenderness and compassion, slow to anger, rich in graciousness, and ready to relent.

Joel 2:12–13

The season of Lent is a time of grace given to us by God, in order to live in a more deliberate and conscious manner that element of Christian life which we call change of heart. It is a time for special effort, of preparation for the celebration of the great feast of Easter, the Resurrection of the Lord. The grace which we shall receive on that day is related to the kind of preparation we make to celebrate it.

In this reading, emphasis is put on the return to God. This is an emphasis of what must always be part of our Christian life, which is a constant change of heart – away from those things that separate us from God, towards those things which unite us to him.

It is not just a question of turning away from what separates us from God, but very much more a question of turning to God, and therefore away from those things that separate us from him.

Therefore in this period of concentration which we call Lent, part of our resolution must be to increase our life of prayer, to make certain that there is, in accordance with the circumstances of our lives, an increase in the time which we spend in prayer. If we do this, then we can be certain that God will speak to us, and guide us, and make increasingly clear to us what it may be in our lives which prevents our having a union with him, which is what he wants, and what, deep down, we want.

❦

Prayer

Father, help me to turn away from those things which separate me from you, to make this Lent a time of turning to you.

Take up your cross
Thursday after Ash Wednesday

Scripture Reading

Then to all he said, 'If anyone wants to be a follower of mine, let him renounce himself and take up his cross every day and follow me. For anyone who wants to save his life will lose it; but anyone who loses his life for my sake, that man will save it.'

Luke 9:23–24

Suffering comes to each one of us. We cannot escape it. It is easy to allow ourselves to become bitter and unhappy. We refuse to accept. We do not try to understand.

Our Lord suffered and died because he wanted to prove his love for us. It is hard to show love when everything that happens to us would tempt us to become bitter and unhappy. Our Lord did it, and so must we. We accept what God allows because we want to prove to him that we love him.

Behind every crucifix stands our risen Lord. Hidden in every suffering and pain is the joy of closer union with him. His is the victory. He invites us to share it. When we are in pain we know only the carrying of the cross. It is only through faith and with the experience of suffering that we will discover the joy of the resurrection that lies deep in the agony of the crucifixion.

※

Prayer

Father, support us and protect us in your loving kindness as we unload our burden of pain and suffering onto you.

'Yes' to God – love of my neighbour

Friday after Ash Wednesday

❧

Scripture Reading

Is not this the sort of fast that pleases me – it is the Lord Yahweh who speaks – to break unjust fetters and undo the thongs of the yoke, to let the oppressed go free, and break every yoke, to share your bread with the hungry, and shelter the homeless poor, to clothe the man you see to be naked and not turn from your own kin?

Isaiah 58:6–7

How wonderful it would be if the love of God was our priority and the love of neighbour flowed from that. Love of neighbour, of fellow human beings, can never be separated from love of God.

We can use almsgiving as an umbrella term to cover all those good things we can do for other people; saying yes to God and yes to my neighbour. It is one aspect of the season of Lent to be consciously aware of our neighbour, and to plan to give of our time, of our affection, of our service.

My interest in homelessness stems from the Christian obligation to help those in need. I believe that we have a duty to look frankly at the social conditions around us and to work to do what we can to address the specific needs which we find.

Homelessness is one of the most pressing of contemporary social problems. Without a home or family surroundings a person lacks something fundamental, deeply affecting. I think of Our Lord looking down now and saying, 'I know what it is to have no home.' To all those who have no proper home, he says, 'I have a special love for you.'

🐝

Prayer

Lord, shelter me in your loving kindness; guide me to live out your justice in the earthly city.

A time for repentance
Saturday after Ash Wednesday

❧

Scripture Reading

The Pharisees and their scribes complained to his disciples and said, 'Why do you eat and drink with tax collectors and sinners?' Jesus said to them in reply, 'It is not those who are well who need the doctor, but the sick. I have not come to call the virtuous, but sinners to repentance.'

Luke 5:30–32

In this time of Lent we have to remind ourselves that we are sinners. There are two ways of thinking about sin: an unhealthy way which leads to depression and discouragement, and a healthy way which leads to true repentance, true sorrow.

And true sorrow for sin always includes with it confidence in God, confidence in his forgiveness, reminding us always that one of the loveliest qualities of God's love is his great desire to forgive. And so it is healthy to say, 'Yes, I am a sinner,' and to recognise that this should lead us to turn to God full of confidence in his love and mercy.

Lent is a time to remind ourselves that we are sinners, to be sorrowful for our sins and to make amends, and to change our way of life so that we can be living more fully and better the life of the gospel.

Make Lent a time of prayer, a time of penance, and a time especially of drawing nearer to God.

✻

Prayer

Lord, we are all sinners; keep us from death, that we may turn to you and eternal life.

Forty days in the desert
First Sunday of Lent

Scripture Reading

Filled with the Holy Spirit, Jesus left the Jordan and was led by the Spirit through the wilderness, being tempted there by the devil for forty days. ... Having exhausted all these ways of tempting him, the devil left him, to return at the appointed time.

Luke 4:1, 13

During Lent, like Christ, we too need to live for forty days in the desert. It is for us a time to attend more closely to God, and to purify our hearts. We prune so that new life may blossom and bear fruit. Today we begin to reflect on the mystery by recalling the three temptations of Christ after his forty days of fasting and prayer. The temptations of Christ reveal the human condition. They tell us something about faith, hope and the sovereignty of God over the whole of creation.

First, the devil took advantage of Christ's hunger to tempt him to limit his concern to the relief of human need. These are vital concerns; but they cannot be the sole concern of the Church. We need daily bread; we need too a reason for living, a sense of purpose, a vision. We need the bread of life, the word of truth which comes from God.

The second temptation was to seek a sign. The children of God have to be prepared to wait in faith and enduring hope. We realise that love alone will conquer hate, and that life is found only in the experience of death. In the darkness we have faith in the light, we hope for life without end. Despair paralyses the human will. Instead, we offer the inspiration of hope and new life.

The final temptation is to use earthly power and strength to compel the good we wish to achieve. In faith and hope we must be content with weakness and apparent failure. It is our task to witness to the truth and commit ourselves to the gospel of reconciliation, peace, unity, love of others. We must be consistent and wholehearted in our service of God.

❧

Prayer

Father, teach me to reject the temptation of sin, to turn rather to serve you and my neighbour, and to fulfil your designs for me.

The poverty of detachment
Monday of the first week of Lent

❦

Scripture Reading

'I was hungry and you gave me food; I was thirsty and you gave me drink; I was a stranger and you made me welcome; naked and you clothed me, sick and you visited me, in prison and you came to see me.'

Matthew 25:35–36

When we read about poverty in the world, hunger and homelessness, illiteracy and conflict, we ought to reflect often how we have been spared these things. It is a matter which frightens me sometimes, that life has been so easy; that we belong to that smaller part of humanity which has not to suffer from these things. And we who live in comfort should recognise that we are part of a privileged minority. But we should recognise too that we have, as Christians, responsibilities towards that part of humanity – by far the largest – which is deprived of so much.

How wrong we would be if, reflecting on the Gospel –

'Lord, when did we see you hungry and feed you...' we were to conclude that our task is to rush off somewhere and start working in hospitals or providing food. No; in the first place, we have to be very deeply aware of these problems.

Our part is to be true to our vocation; to be unworldly in our bearing, our behaviour, our speech; to be aware of that aspect of poverty which is detachment, unworldliness. To be true to our vocation means spiritual values, so that it is clear to all that we live for God. We cannot allow ourselves to live an inward-looking life, ignoring the very true needs of the world today.

✤

Prayer

Father, give us true poverty of heart and spirit as we turn our hearts and minds to you.

Prayer in the secret of the heart
Tuesday of the first week of Lent

❧

Scripture Reading

'When you pray, go to your private room, and pray to your Father who is in that secret place, and your Father who sees all that is done in secret will reward you. Do not babble as the pagans do, for they think that by using many words they will make themselves heard.'

Matthew 6:6–7

Obviously one of the great dangers of a busy life is that we can become so busy that we can very easily fail to have an interior life. It is one of the things that terrifies me – that we can live this life day after day, month after month, year after year, and not really be a deep person. We can find ourselves becoming all the time interiorly superficial and living almost hypocritically.

So easy to talk about religion and not have any religion; to give advice we would not take ourselves; to be eloquent for the things of God, and have no warmth for the things of God.

It is a very real danger, the danger of the absence of a deep prayerful attitude. When we lose the nostalgia for prayer; when we look back over the day and find we have done no more than we had to; we may be dangerously close to losing a sense of God. They are important things, but easy for us to lose.

If we decide this Lent to make no more effort than to deepen the life we live with God in secret, that would be a Lent well spent.

❧

Prayer

Father, help me to turn to you in prayer. Hear the prayers which I make to you in the secret of my heart.

Acknowledging weakness leads to peace

Wednesday of the first week of Lent

❧

Scripture Reading

The people of Nineveh believed in God; they pro-
claimed a fast and put on sackcloth, from the
greatest to the least ... God saw their efforts to
renounce their evil behaviour. And God relented.

Jonah 3:5, 10

It would be a very strange person indeed who was
totally unaware of the imperfection that is in each
one of us; very strange if we did not realise that in
fact we belong to a sinful humanity and that there is a
flaw in each one of us. It would be very curious if we did
not realise that at times we say things, do things, or omit
things of which – when we reflect on them – we are
ashamed.

Shame is no bad motive, if not the highest, but more
important is to realise that so often in our lives we are
displeasing to God. It is good to admit our sinfulness,
our weakness, and to confess it. It is a fact of experience,

is it not, that when we are honest with ourselves and admit our weakness and sinfulness, there comes a deep peace.

These thoughts are very apt as we begin this season of penance, providing us with an opportunity to reflect on our weakness and sinfulness, to admit and confess it, and to realise that our Lord came to give us his forgiveness; an opportunity to dwell on that thought and to understand and prepare for that great week which we call Holy Week and for the great Feast for which we are already preparing – the resurrection of our Lord and all the joy that can bring. Our preparation for that is this long period of Lent when we turn from what separates us from God to that which unites, through prayer, penance and self-denial.

❦

Prayer

Father, forgive my sin. Fill me with love for you, and renew my heart and mind that I may turn back to you.

The solidarity of all humanity
Thursday of the first week of Lent

❧

Scripture Reading

Always treat others as you would like them to treat you; that is the meaning of the Law and the Prophets.

Matthew 7:12

What is solidarity based on? It is based first of all on the oneness of that humanity which we all share. Made to the image and likeness of God, and each one of us totally unique, unrepeatable. Each person with whom we come into contact can tell us something about God which nobody else can. Part of the art of living with other people is to try to discover that what makes them loveable to God must make them loveable to me.

It is on these thoughts that we base the dignity of each person. The dignity of each person is based on the fact that that person, made to the image and likeness of God is totally unique and can tell me something about God which nobody else can. Because that person has such a great dignity, then that person has rights, which we call human rights.

The human right to freedom, to food and drink, freedom of thought, freedom of speech. Human rights are many. But not only are there rights, but also what goes with them – responsibilities. Responsibility to others and for others, to promote other people's rights, to fight to preserve other people's dignity. We are talking about solidarity.

There is a oneness among us all in virtue of the fact that we are just human. This is what is at the heart of the Gospel.

❧

Prayer

Lord, help me, today and always, to seek your image in everyone I meet, everyone I speak to.

God's unrequited love
Friday of the first week of Lent

❦

Scripture Reading

Thus says the Lord God, 'If the wicked man renounces all the sins he has committed, respects my laws and is law-abiding and honest, he will certainly live; he will not die.'

Ezekiel 18:21

God is like a lover who loves and whose love is not returned. So he has to wait, and he waits for a change of heart in his beloved. He waits, and he does not force, because to force would be to violate the law of love. He waits until the strength of his love begins to dawn on the one whom he loves and who is not yet able to return it. And he reveals himself this way, hoping that the beloved will begin to open his eyes and ears to what God has done.

This change of heart in the beloved, you and me, is conversion. This conversion, this change of heart, includes repentance. Repentance is not repentance for a

Christian unless it includes the realisation of forgiveness. If it did not, it would be shame or remorse.

But for the Christian, sorrow for our sins, a realisation of our weakness, is never depressing, should never make us downcast, because if it is truly the result of the grace of God then at the same time it includes the dawning, the realisation of what his forgiveness is. So repentance for the Christian is always, paradoxically, a joyous occasion, one that leads to peace.

❧

Prayer

Father, as we turn our hearts and minds to you, give us the peace of your forgiveness.

Preparing for perfection
Saturday of the first week of Lent

✣

Scripture Reading

'I say this to you: love your enemies and pray for
those who persecute you; in this way you will be
children of your Father in heaven ... For if you love
those who love you, what reward will you get? ...
You must be perfect just as your heavenly Father is
perfect.'

Matthew 5:44, 46, 48

The commandment to love God is clear, and we
are furthermore expected to put our whole selves
into it. It is easy enough to give notional assent to
this proposition, but *real* assent, and translated into a
programme of action, is quite another thing.

We must understand clearly what is meant. We so
often distort the concept of love; we caricature the
reality; we deface it; we think of it as a weak, rather
insipid, emotion. But the love of which the Lord speaks
is demanding. It is a giving experience, selfless and
generous. It wants to give as much as it wants to receive;

and its model and the prototype is the love as it is in God. We study this love of God by looking at the actions and the attitudes of his divine Son.

'Be perfect as your heavenly Father is perfect.' If we are to love God and our neighbour, then we must be constantly changing, because we do not, and never will, function as we should. Pride and self-centredness ruin not only the lives of others, but our own too. So I see this present life as a period of training, a time of preparation during which we learn the art of loving God and our neighbour.

Religion without the love of God is cold and unreal, it becomes burdensome. The love of God, love of our neighbours: *that* is the heart of it all. It is the secret which we must all discover for ourselves. Nothing can take the place of my own personal and individual search for God and his love.

❧

Prayer

God our Father, train us to discover you in our neighbour, through our love for you.

A cheerful, joyous love
Second Sunday of Lent

❧

Scripture Reading

Our homeland is in heaven, and from heaven comes the saviour we are waiting for, the Lord Jesus Christ, and he will transfigure these wretched bodies of ours into copies of his glorious body.

Philippians 3:20–21

Lent is a time during which we should look forward to the celebrations of Holy Week, that is, to the joy of Easter, the triumph of Christ our Lord over death and over sin. That is our great joy – that is the foundation of all our hope. But there is another looking forward which is part of Christian living and one to which we turn our attention in particular during Lent, and it is the looking forward to heaven, to the time when we shall be totally, wholly with God.

A turning to God. Therefore, how important it is in planning our Lent that there should be resolutions of a very positive nature. Turning away from what separates us from God. The most dangerous thing is pride: I will not serve; I make myself the centre of my life; I want my way; I want things to go the way I think they ought to. The second great sin is unkindness – lack of charity, lack of love. There is a third thing that separates us from God, which you might find surprising – grumbling.

I learnt this from the Rule of St Benedict, which is constantly telling monks that they must not be grumblers. This is very shrewd. There is nothing worse than living with people who grumble; there is nothing more corrosive than grumbling; nothing more unsettling than grumbling.

Let our Lent be not only cheerful but deeply joyous, because we have determined to turn to God, and we know that to turn to God is to receive an outpouring of his love.

❦

Prayer

Lord, turn our hearts and minds away from ourselves, towards you.

The generosity of love
Monday of the second week of Lent

✤

Scripture Reading

Jesus said to his disciples, 'Be compassionate as your Father is compassionate ... Give, and there will be gifts for you: a full measure, pressed down, shaken together, and running over, will be poured into your lap; because the amount you measure out is the amount you will be given back.'

Luke 6:36, 38

I have found again and again a visit to a hospital to be as instructive and inspiring as a good sermon or a spiritual book. I have seen patience, courage and cheerfulness amidst great pain and sorrow. Suffering patiently and courageously borne can not only bring the best out of a person, but can also enable that person to reflect more insistently on the meaning and purpose of life.

There is in each one of us a conflict and it is one seldom totally resolved. It is a conflict between two tendencies. One is the tendency to pursue our own interests at the expense of those of other people. We call it selfishness. The other is to spend ourselves in the service of others even at great cost. We call it generosity. The final victory of the latter, generosity, over the former, selfishness, is generally the result of small daily triumphs of thoughtfulness and selflessness.

Compassion, generosity's closest companion must be acquired. Compassion can often be underdeveloped; sometimes it is stifled by the pressures to succeed, or the instinct to think only of personal desires, irrespective of the needs of others.

To give is, paradoxically, also to receive. If the cost is great the payment exceeds it. The reward for self-sacrifice is to be found deep within us, and at a depth which only God can see. Furthermore, is it not a fact that those who are generous and compassionate are much loved and respected by those whose needs have been met, who have been comforted in their pain, consoled in their loneliness, or accompanied when frightened and bewildered?

❦

Prayer

Father, fill us with your compassion; give us the generosity to spend ourselves for others.

A conversion towards the kingdom of God

Tuesday of the second week of Lent

❧

Scripture Reading

'Take your wrong-doing out of my sight. Cease to do evil. Learn to do good, search for justice, help the oppressed, be just to the orphan, plead for the widow. Come now, let us talk this over, says Yahweh. Though your sins are like scarlet, they shall be as white as snow; though they are red as crimson, they shall be like wool.'

Isaiah 1:16–18

I never cease to be distressed at the pain and suffering which we humans can inflict on each other. The second commandment of our Lord is to love our neighbour as ourselves. I sometimes think it must sound naïve, and a bit too unworldly, to speak of basing a social and political system on mutual love. Maybe it is naïve to think of basing it on anything else. Surely the opposite of love is hatred, self-assertion, jealousy, rivalry – and these do not make for peace.

Let me be clear: the love about which I am speaking is not something limp, a matter of vaguely liking another, or an emotional involvement, or a feeling. It is, rather, a demanding taskmaster; it will require me to love my enemy.

It effects a change of heart – away from what separates us from God – violence, cruelty, murder – and with a turning to him. The kingdom of God takes root in proportion as the citizens of the city of humanity turn from evil to God. Now, there is no turning to God which is not a search to understanding the meaning of love, as he shows it to us, and which we should have for him. And that cannot be separated from the love which we must have and show towards each other. This twofold commandment is the heart of the Gospel.

❦

Prayer

Father, as we turn to you, help us to understand the meaning of love, to love you and our neighbour more and more each day.

A share in Christ's Passion
Wednesday of the second week of Lent

❧

Scripture Reading

The mother of Zebedee's sons said to him, 'Promise that these two sons of mine may sit one at your right hand and the other at your left in your kingdom'. 'You do not know what you are asking', Jesus answered. 'Can you drink the cup that I am going to drink?' They replied, 'We can.' 'Very well,' he said, 'you shall drink my cup.'

Matthew 20:21–23

Often, we are called upon to share in the Passion of Christ; in very small ways, each day; the various difficulties, contradictions, misunderstandings, and so forth; and at times there can be long periods of stress and strain, periods of sadness and sorrow, in which we truly are living the Passion of Christ in our lives.

Now, such suffering is purposeful and valuable – it has a value precisely because Christ has risen from the dead, precisely because he has overcome all that is negative in suffering, and given it a particular value, since each sharing in the Passion of Christ leads us to a greater sharing in the life of his resurrection.

It is purposeful at different levels – first of all, it saves us from deceiving ourselves into thinking that achievement in this world is the thing that really matters, and reminds us that our treasure is in heaven. Every difficulty in life is a call from God to turn one's attention to him, and to try to find in him the ultimate meaning of our lives. Secondly, at a mystical level: by meditating on the Passion of Christ we grow in sympathy for, and understanding of, what he did for us.

It has always been a Christian instinct in times of stress and difficulty to recognise that one is participating in the Passion of Christ, and that this is good, in that it draws one closer to him.

❧

Prayer

Father, help us to turn our suffering to positive love for you, and lead us to share in Christ's resurrection.

Accepting what comes our way
Thursday of the second week of Lent

Scripture Reading

'There was a rich man who used to dress in purple and fine linen and feast magnificently every day. And at his gate there lay a poor man called Lazarus, covered with sores, who longed to fill himself with the scraps that fell from the rich man's table.'

Luke 16:19–20

The practices which we undertake in Lent – the self-denials – seem often to be negative, a masochistic approach, less than human, too negative. I think it is just worth pointing out that life is full of frustrations, of sorrows, of pain, and when it comes our way – as inevitably it does – we instinctively recoil from it, hide from it, escape from it. It is natural that we should.

It does help if from time to time we accept consciously some sadness, frustration or pain – even, indeed, impose it on ourselves so that when it is meted out to us through the ordinary processes of living we recognise it for what it is and learn to cope with it.

During the course of the year we have missed many opportunities in the service of God, through selfishness, through self-seeking, through pettiness. Lent is a time when we do something almost unreasonable from one point of view in order to try to make amends.

More important, the small things that we undertake, or the deeper acceptance of the things that come our way, make us realise our solidarity with our fellow Christians, indeed with our fellow men, the vast majority of whom are men and women of sorrow. It is difficult to remember that we live in the most pampered part of God's world. It is very difficult for us to remember constantly just how roughly life treats the majority of our fellow men and women. And it is good to want to live or be in solidarity with them in Christ.

❦

Prayer

Lord, help us to offer you our Lenten sacrifice as a solidarity with our brothers and sisters.

Hope, forgiveness, love
Friday of the second week of Lent

❦

Scripture Reading

The spirit of the Lord Yahweh has been given to me, for Yahweh has anointed me. He has sent me to bring good news to the poor, to bind up hearts that are broken; to proclaim liberty to captives, freedom to those in prison.

Isaiah 61:1

Christ came for all of us, for all are in need, and all are in need of healing. But by singling out the poor, the captives, the broken-hearted, the oppressed, he was laying particular stress on a special characteristic of his ministry, namely his special concern for what today we would call the 'marginalised'; those who, for one reason or another, have been pushed to the margins of our society: the economically poor, the homeless, the elderly, those mistakenly considered to have little or nothing to contribute to our society.

The good news is a word of hope. There is no situation

that is so dark nor apparently so irretrievable that would justify hope being a stranger.

The good news is a word of forgiveness. For those who repent sincerely, of course, but also for those caught up in complex situations and who try, often in spite of themselves and unaware, to let the good in them overcome the wrong that has become a habit.

The good news is a word of love. Too few of us really believe in the warmth and intimacy of God's love for us.

A word that gives hope; a word of forgiveness; a word that speaks of God's love: are not these wonderful ways of speaking about God? These are words to encourage; they are indeed good news.

※

Prayer

Father, teach us to speak about the hope, the forgiveness and the love which you offer to each person.

He was lost, and is found
Saturday of the second week of Lent

❧

Scripture Reading

While he was still a long way off, his father saw him and was moved with pity. He ran to the boy, clasped him in his arms and kissed him tenderly. Then his son said, 'Father, I have sinned against heaven and against you. I no longer deserve to be called your son.' But the father said to his servants, 'We are going to have a celebration, because this son of mine was lost and is found.'

Luke 15:20–24

We are told here about a young man who leaves home, claiming his inheritance, and then proceeds to squander it 'on a life of debauchery'. Perhaps he had been caught up in the brambles and briars of life, that is, in things he thought would give him a quick reward, but which turned out to make him their prisoner and hold him fast. And the more he fought to be free, the stronger their grip became. There is no need for me to list those things that so easily captivate us and then make us their captives – quick returns, but long-term disasters.

The Lord had been criticised for mixing with the wrong people – 'this man welcomes sinners and eats with them'. So Jesus set out to explain what sort of person his Father was. He was telling us something very important about God.

Note especially the reaction of the boy's father when he spotted him on his way home. This, I believe, is the most astonishing explanation – or revelation – of what God is like. Just thinking about that verse can, quite simply, transform our lives. Think of God moved with pity for you, of God wanting to embrace you, of him just wanting you. This is the language of love, is it not; but make no mistake about it, it is the language of God.

❦

Prayer

Father, help us to turn away from those things which captivate us, to turn our love and our attention to you.

A thirst for God's justice
Third Sunday of Lent

❦

Scripture Reading

Jesus replied: 'Whoever drinks this water will get thirsty again; but anyone who drinks the water that I shall give will never be thirsty again: the water that I shall give will turn into a spring inside him, welling up to eternal life.'

John 4:13–15

The thirst for significant religious experience is indeed characteristic of many today. They seek a God who is real and immediate; they want an experience and belief that matters to them and gives results here and now. This yearning for a direct encounter with God is a precious gift; it is proof of God's enduring and transforming presence in ourselves and in our world. The danger, however, is that experience and feeling come and go. What excited last year is sterile and banal today.

Christianity, it must be said, is based on revelation; but to receive revelation requires humility, trust and openness. Believers must so absorb revelation into themselves that it becomes a seed of life and love, transforming their whole being. They believe and so they can experience something of transcendent reality.

Among the signs of life and love present in people today there is the persistent thirst for experience of God. There is also a more widespread awareness of human solidarity. Isolationism is still to be found, of course, but increasingly individuals recognise the claims of justice and react with compassion as never before to the victims of hunger, injustice and deprivation. Concern for the victims of natural disasters, famine and drought is a comparatively recent phenomenon and represents a significant personal growth in human consciousness worldwide.

The building of the kingdom of God in the city of man requires energy, patience and involvement. We cannot simply wait for the kingdom to happen, we have to pray for it ceaselessly and work for it tirelessly and recognise its every manifestation in the affairs of humanity.

❦

Prayer

Lord, satisfy our thirst for you; fill us with thirst for your justice.

Awareness of God's presence
Monday of the third week of Lent

❧

Scripture Reading

How my soul yearns and pines for Yahweh's courts!
My heart and my flesh sing for joy to the living God.

Psalm 84:2

There is in human make-up a fundamental need for
God. There is, too, a restlessness of the mind,
always in search of truth, for ultimate meaning,
for knowledge and reasons. It will only be when all is
known and love is secure, that we shall be at rest.

That experience of love totally fulfilled belongs to the
future, to our being in another situation, where there
will be nothing for any of us save the immediacy of the
vision of God. Meanwhile we try to achieve some
'awareness' of God and his presence within us. To set
out on that pilgrimage of discovery and search will
involve, always, that radical change of heart which is
involved when we turn to God.

Where then do we begin to look to find God, or at
least to catch a glimpse of him? Do we hear his voice

calling to us, or at any rate listen to the echo of his call? We do not, of course, see him as he truly is, nor do we hear his voice clear and compelling.

We can see now only something of God, know him in his work, as the artist in his creation. We can listen to his word, the scriptures; we can find him, too in those deep experiences of joy or pain. Above all there is his Word, the Word that became flesh. Thus in creation, in the scriptures, in Jesus Christ, we seek God and see something of him or hear the echo of his voice. At the very centre of our being, we have a sense of his presence as he becomes part of our awareness and the object of our desiring.

❧

Prayer

Father, teach us to recognise your presence, to turn to you when we hear your voice.

In the image and likeness of God
Tuesday of the third week of Lent

Scripture Reading

'The master sent for him. "You wicked servant," he said "I cancelled all that debt of yours when you appealed to me. Were you not bound, then, to have pity on your fellow servant, just as I had pity on you?" And in his anger, the master handed him over to the torturers till he should pay all his debt. And that is how my heavenly Father will deal with you unless you each forgive your brother from your heart.'

Matthew 18:32–35

We believe that every human being is made in the image and likeness of God and, therefore, possesses a dignity and value which can never be taken away. We believe that as children of the one God we are one family, with mutual responsibility for each other. We treasure life as God's most precious gift and seek to defend it and enhance it.

The Church has come to realise over the centuries

that individual compassion and generosity can never meet the needs of the suffering world. We must examine and change the processes and structures of the world which at present promote division and ultimately bring death. We must turn them into mechanisms of international collaboration and human solidarity, and ultimately into sources of life.

Today our brothers are not looking for a keeper, but for a caring and sharing brother. So what would such a caring and sharing brother or sister set out to tackle today? The stranglehold of international debt must be loosened. Debt is bringing death in its wake. We used to call the extortion of excessive interest 'usury'; it was condemned in scripture and in church tradition. Is it less evil today?

※

Prayer

Lord, help us to bring life to our brothers and sisters by loosening the stranglehold of debt.

Genuine human freedom
Wednesday of the third week of Lent

❧

Scripture Reading

See, as Yahweh my God has commanded me, I teach you the laws and customs that you are to observe and make your own. Keep them, observe them, and they will demonstrate to the peoples your wisdom and understanding.

Deuteronomy 4:5–6

A re the moral requirements of the Scriptures an imposition, a constraint upon human freedom? Genuine human freedom, it is argued, requires us to determine our own moral codes, not submit to those of others.

Morality presupposes freedom. Unless I can genuinely choose, and unless I have some knowledge or awareness of what it is I am choosing, I cannot be held morally responsible for my actions. Morality presupposes a basic moral awareness, that good should be done and evil avoided. The crucial question in society today is: who decides 'the good'?

There are still, of course, some widely held moral standards. Basic values such as honesty, kindness, generosity, consideration for others, compassion, faithfulness in relationships and respect for human life are shared by very many people.

Moral responsibility requires each of us to exercise our own judgement. We are not left orphans. We are guided, but God does not decide for us. We cannot escape from the dignity of responsibility through blind or unthinking obedience. In the muddle and complexity of many practical situations we are entrusted with the responsibility of moral choice.

Our part is to use the gift of that freedom by always seeking to choose wisely and well, in conformity with objective moral norms.

※

Prayer

Father, guide us to use our freedom wisely by choosing our actions well.

A share in the divine life
Thursday of the third week of Lent

❧

Scripture Reading

'Listen to my voice, then I will be your God and you
shall be my people ... But they did not listen, they
did not pay attention; they followed the dictates of
their own evil hearts, refused to face me, and
turned their backs on me.'

Jeremiah 7:25

Ours is the choice to live dead, to live separated
from God, but if we choose to live for him,
then we live with that life which Christ gives
us. But our Lord must be constantly at work on us all the
time. His saving power must always be operating in our
regard in order to check those forces which make for
separation from God.

Our natural life is sustained by a constant willing by
God. Were God one moment to cease to will us, we
would return to the nothingness from which we came. If
that is so of natural life, how much more true will it be
of that life with which we have been recreated in Christ.

His life-giving touch is held out constantly to us and we, of course, can always refuse to be touched.

What did our Lord do by his Passion, death and resurrection? He was, of course, bridging that gulf which exists between God and man, a gulf which can only be bridged by him. He is the mediator standing between God and man for the precise reason that he is both God and man. But at his death he was giving to God his father on the cross all that is human; at the same time he was giving to man, or would give to man, a share in the divine life. It is the role of Christ to give to God the things of man, and to give to man the things of God. Thus the passion, death and resurrection are the central points of all history, and each individual person must be brought into contact with that work of Christ.

❦

Prayer

Lord, help us to focus on the share in the divine life which you have won for us.

Truly seeking God's will
Friday of the third week of Lent

❧

Scripture Reading

'You must love the Lord your God with all your
heart, with all your soul, with all your mind and
with all your strength; you must love your neighbour as yourself. There is no commandment greater
than these.'

Mark 12:29–30

St Benedict tells us that in Lent we have to apply
ourselves, which in simple terms means making an
extra and special effort, not so much to do
extraordinary things, but rather to concentrate on getting the ordinary things right.

One area where we can usefully examine ourselves at
this period is in the area of our relationships with others.
We ought to consider whether we do treat others with
that courtesy, civility, generosity, sensitivity and understanding that is necessary, and whether the needs of
others are more important to us than our own personal
needs.

More important still in this time is the fact that we must face up to our attitude to our service of God. Are we truly seeking him; do we really want to do his will; do we really accept his will as it is translated to us in the daily circumstances of our living; do we really see his will in those things which can happen to us – the difficulties, the frustrations; do we really want what he wants; do we really want God's will, God's way, or are we always seeking God's will *our* way?

Prayer

Father, give me the courage and humility to truly seek to do your will, through my love for you and my neighbour.

God, be merciful to me, a sinner
Saturday of the third week of Lent

🌿

Scripture Reading

'Two men went up to the Temple to pray ... The
tax collector stood some distance away, not daring
even to raise his eyes to heaven; but he beat his
breast and said, "God be merciful to me, a sinner."
This man, I tell you, went home again at rights with
God.'

Luke 18:10, 13–14

The message our Lord gives us is the message of
love. The way he touches us with the Sacraments
is the gesture of a lover. With this in mind I read
to you now a favourite passage. Everyone, as we go
through life, becomes increasingly aware of our frailty.
We become increasingly conscious that in some way we
are failures. We are not responding to him as he would
wish, and as we know deep down we should.

'Two men went up to the Temple to pray ... The
Pharisee stood there and said this prayer to himself, "I
thank you God, that I am not grasping, unjust,

adulterous like the rest of mankind ... I fast twice a week, I pay tithes on all I get." '

No man can boast and be able to say: I have never committed adultery, I don't cheat, I don't steal, I fast. That man does not find favour with God. This is the great passage now coming.

'The tax collector stood some distance away, not daring even to raise his eyes to heaven; but he beat his breast and said, "God, be merciful to me a sinner." '

Nothing else need be said. He admitted it, and he had nothing which could make favour with God, except – and this is the *marvellous* thing – his weakness, his inadequacy, his failures, his nothingness.

Every man or woman who humbles himself, herself, shall please him. Isn't that marvellous, to be able to say: I am a sinner, be merciful to me. Just for a moment, let us quietly relate, identify, with that tax collector. I do, because it is quite easy.

❧

Prayer

God, be merciful to me, a sinner. Accept my weakness, inadequacy, failures as an offering to you.

In search of God
Fourth Sunday of Lent

❦

Scripture Reading

'While he was still a long way off, his father saw him
and was moved with pity. He ran to the boy,
clasped him in his arms and kissed him tenderly.
Then his son said, "Father, I have sinned against
heaven and against you. I no longer deserve to be
called your son." But the father said to his servants,
"We are going to have a celebration, because this
son of mine was lost and is found."'

Luke 15:20–24

I have long believed, and often said, that humanity is
all the time in search of God, though often we do
not know it. But, in so far as we are searching for
truth, for goodness, for beauty, and in so far as we are in
search of love, of justice, of happiness, then we are in
search of God. If we live those search experiences, so I
believe, we catch a glimpse of God.

Humanity is in search of God, but only because God
is in search of humanity. It is always that way round, for

in every case, and at every moment, the initiative is always his.

Can anything be more moving, more consoling, than this little scene, which speaks so eloquently of the way God sees and understands each one of us? Just think of those words – your Father sees you, takes pity on you, and, running up, will throw his arms around your neck and kiss you.

The Father is in search of us always, his wayward sons and daughters. But as we pursue our search for God, we shall, as the search progresses, discover Christ. Wounded though we are, lost though we often seem to be, mistaken many a time in the way we should search and serve, nonetheless we come back always to him.

❦

Prayer

Father, help me to search for you in every part of my life, as you search for me always.

Make holy the actions of every day

Monday of the fourth week of Lent

❦

Scripture Reading

For now I create new heavens and a new earth. Be glad and rejoice for ever and ever for what I am creating, because I now create Jerusalem 'Joy' and her people 'Gladness'. I shall rejoice over Jerusalem and exult in my people.

Isaiah 65:17–19

We need Christians who will live their faith and be witnesses to truth. Our mission is to make holy our everyday actions, whether at home or at work. This is not often really appreciated. We forget too easily that genuine holiness lies in carrying out God's will wherever we are, whatever we do, at home or at work. That is how we give witness to Gospel values – by the manner of our living and working.

All are sons and daughters of God, equal members of the family of God. All have a right to their fair share of the world's resources. All must be treated as cherished brothers and sisters. Those who suffer or are deprived of their rights should be able to look to us to campaign for their rights and tend to their injuries. Some would argue that this social and human concern is no part of Christian belief, no consequence of Christian love. But I am convinced that the prayerful study of the Gospel leads us inevitably and legitimately to Christian action.

We are called to build the kingdom of God within the kingdom of man. This causes us to wrestle with some of the most intractable problems and menacing dangers of our time. The struggle for the kingdom is not an abstract conflict. It has to be fought here and now, in conditions dictated by history and contemporary needs. And so we have to contend with the problems of our age, while we try, as best we can, to empty ourselves of the will to dominate, and rely instead on the invincible power of divine love. We must be ready to dialogue and be flexible. We must never lose patience or hope. We must be ready to initiate and be positive, not simply to react defensively and belatedly.

✣

Prayer

Lord, help me to quietly carry out your will in my everyday tasks, to witness through this to the Gospel message.

The ultimate value of each person
Tuesday of the fourth week of Lent

❧

Scripture Reading

For my part, I look to Yahweh, my hope is in the
God who will save me; my God will hear me ... he
takes up my cause and rights my wrongs; he will
bring me out into the light and I shall rejoice to see
the rightness of his ways.

Micah 7:7–9

In our society we are sometimes encouraged to judge
people exclusively by what they achieve, by their
jobs, their wealth, their position, even where they
live. Therefore, to have no job, to be poor, to be old, to
suffer from a chronic illness, or to be without a home –
any and all of these can make a person feel useless and
rejected, of no value to society, and a burden on others.

We are each made in the image and likeness of God
and specifically elected by him just to 'be', to exist.
Every individual must be given every opportunity to live
a life in which his or her basic needs are provided for,

and in which so far as is reasonably possible, his or her full potential is realised. Each person matters. No human life is ever redundant. Indeed, the Gospels tell us that it is particularly in those who are pushed to the margins that Christ is to be found.

Sadly, homelessness is still a pressing social problem throughout the country. For many, it seems that there is no sense of hope. Yet behind each face is a personal story, the circumstances that brought that individual person to this state. These people are precious in the eyes of God, and thus must be precious in ours.

It is hard to exaggerate the importance of a decent home – somewhere that is not just a temporary roof but which can be a place of security and safety – where a person can grow and develop. Those who work to ensure this symbolise a truth about the ultimate value of each person, made in the image and likeness of God.

🦋

Prayer

Father, turn me away from judging others to seeing your image in them.

God searching for us
Wednesday of the fourth week of Lent

❧

Scripture Reading

Zion was saying, 'Yahweh has abandoned me, the Lord has forgotten me.' ... Even if these forget, I will never forget you.

Isaiah 49:14, 15

Whenever we try to speak about God we always have to do so with great reverence, remembering that we understand very little about him. He is far too great for our small minds to have anything but the beginning of an idea. We know so little about him, other than what he has told us himself.

God has spoken: he spoke a word and created the world, made the sun, the moon, the stars, the sea, the whole earth. Above all, he spoke a word and created us, made to his image and likeness. He goes on speaking about himself through the things he has made; they are his messages about himself, so that in all that is good, beautiful, we have a glimpse of him.

God spoke his special Word – the Word that became

flesh and dwelt among us, the image of the invisible God, Jesus Christ, true God and true man. We need to spread the good news of the Gospel, and at the heart of it is Jesus Christ, true God and true man, who tells us in all that he said and did what God is like. In the whole of the life of our Lord, all that he said, all that he did, is the working out of what Isaiah records: God searching for us, God in love with us, God wanting to be in touch with us.

※

Prayer

Father, help us to find you in the beauty of your whole creation, through which you teach us of your love for us.

False gods
Thursday of the fourth week of Lent

❧

Scripture Reading

Then Yahweh spoke to Moses, 'Go down now,
because your people whom you brought out of
Egypt have apostasised. They have been quick to
leave the way I marked out for them; they have
made themselves a calf of molten metal and have
worshipped it and offered it sacrifice.'

Exodus 32:7–8

Even in this very secular and Godless age, the
search for God, the incessant yet often unrecog-
nised desire for him, leads many along strange
paths, but even waywardness in the life of the spirit can
point to profound truths.

People sometimes respond to their need for meaning
and fulfilment by pursuing what quickly proves to be a
delusion. We have all been too easily led astray by false
philosophies and unreal promises of a paradise in this
world.

People sometimes rely on drugs to cope with stress

and meaninglessness and to widen their sensory experience. It is an attempt to force an entry into the world of the spirit which is doomed to frustration because it does physical and psychological violence to the personality and leads ultimately to frustration. God's grace always builds upon nature, it never violates it.

There are, of course, innumerable signs of the denial of God, among them the pursuit of power, of riches, of uncontrolled pleasure – each of these can so dominate our minds and hearts that we turn them into false gods. We make them ends to be pursued for their own sakes, not means to achieve other and better goods.

But the instinct to pursue that which we see to be best for ourselves is deep and strong. It is an instinct that may move us, when we heed its nobler prompting, to look for a treasure which is proof against corruption. That instinct is the effect of the need for something which is greater and nobler than 'ourselves'; the treasure is God himself.

※

Prayer

Lord, turn us away from the false gods we love and adore, to adore and love you, the one true God.

Our burdens lead to life
Friday of the fourth week of Lent

❧

Scripture Reading

'If the virtuous man is God's son, God will take his part and rescue him from the clutches of his enemies.'. . . They do not know the hidden things of God, they have no hope that holiness will be rewarded, they can see no reward for blameless souls.

Wisdom 2:18, 22

Each of us has a burden to carry; if not today's burden, at least to recall yesterday's, or prepare inevitably for some burden tomorrow, for that is the way of life. There is no human life that does not have its burdens. Much of our lives is indeed the way of the cross, or at least it is so at times.

That burden may be a sorrow, or an anxiety; a broken heart; a secret fear; a chronic pain; a disappointment; a frustration; a wound from the past. Burdens take different shapes and are of varying weights but they have this in common: they press hard on us causing us sometimes to falter and stumble. They make our journey through life more difficult and perhaps at times seemingly impossible and lead us to wonder about the meaning and purpose of it all. That is, until we remember that the burdens we carry always lead to life, life hidden with Christ in God.

All those burdens we carry are crosses which he asks us to carry, and we carry our crosses through life as he carried his. We meet him in a marvellous manner when we help him to carry his burden and he helps us to carry ours.

The sharing of his Passion is the most certain way of growing closer to him and a sure way too of discovering the meaning of the resurrection, the knowledge that whatever befalls us, whatever happens, we can never be separated from love of him.

※

Prayer

Lord, help me to unite the burden I carry to your cross, to carry your cross with you, to allow you to carry my burden with me.

A God of tenderness and compassion

Saturday of the fourth week of Lent

❧

Scripture Reading

Yahweh, Yahweh, a God of tenderness and compassion, slow to anger, rich in kindness and faithfulness; for thousands he maintains his kindness,
forgives faults, transgression, sin.

Exodus 34:6

Compassion, where it is truest, noblest, most
beautiful, most loving, is in God himself. There
we find the example, the model, the inspiration.
One day I discovered in the Bible the word 'mercy',
the mercy of God. I leaned that God is love, and if God
is love, then God is compassion – the two terms are
interchangeable.

There is no finer way of showing compassion than to
give yourself to others, and at the heart of that giving
there will always be acceptance of the other. The compassion which we show to other people has to be mod-
elled on and inspired by the compassion which God first

shows to us. Indeed, the truth is deeper. We become the vehicles, the instruments of God's compassion. Every time we open ourselves to the needs of others, he uses us to show them the meaning of love. That is at the heart of everything; that is the Good News that we have to spread. God who is love has compassion, and orders us to love our neighbours as ourselves.

In practice we have to learn to be compassionate when we are young. It doesn't start in the third world, it doesn't start in the community, it starts in the home. That is were we learn to be compassionate; to be concerned for the old, concerned for the sick, concerned for the handicapped, concerned for the poor, the marginal. They are not 'over there', but next door or in our own home. We have to show compassion there too. It starts in the home.

❦

Prayer

Father, as you are tender and compassionate towards us, teach us to love our neighbour with tenderness and compassion.

Make time for prayer
Fifth Sunday of Lent

❧

Scripture Reading

This is the covenant I will make with the house of Israel when those days arrive. Deep within them I will plant my Law, writing it on their hearts. Then I will be their God and they shall be my people. There will be no further need for neighbour to try to teach neighbour, or brother to say to brother, 'Learn to know Yahweh!' No, they will all know me.

Jeremiah 31:33–34

Prayer is worth doing for its own sake. Any time or effort spent in prayer is well spent. Our Lord used to slip away from the crowds to pray to his Father alone. He made time in his busy life for this. We all need space and time to give ourselves to prayer during the course of the day and the week. Friendships grow by two persons being together or doing things together; if they keep apart, friendship becomes weak, and the friends become strangers. God must never be a stranger.

Many of us have to make an effort to pray. We have to

make time; we have to find out how to do it; we have to keep going when we do not seem to be getting anywhere. But gradually, if we persevere, we get the taste for it, and then we find that we really do want to pray.

There is no real substitute for that prayer which I do when I am alone with God, either trying to speak to the Father, or when I am just silent, knowing that he is present. But prayer together is also important; 'where two or three are gathered in my name, I am there in their midst'. There is nothing like praying together to draw closer to each other. It forms a bond. So a Christian's prayer is two-fold: it is a private, individual matter, and it is something we do together.

※

Prayer

Lord, teach me to spend time with you in prayer; let my prayer develop into true friendship with you.

Divine love, divine judgement
Monday of the fifth week of Lent

Scripture Reading

Jesus replied ... 'You judge by human standards; I judge no one, but if I judge my judgement will be sound, because I am not alone.'

John 8:15–16

Sometimes we are puzzled about how we are to love God. We do not see him with our eyes, we do not touch him with our hands. How can we love him? And yet the command is there, to love him. We can only begin to do that when we begin to realise that the command to love God has to be our response, our answer, our reaction to the love which he has for us.

So we begin always, or should do, when we think about God, by thinking of the great love he has for us, which our Lord came to show us in the way he treated the sick, the way he helped the weak, the way he acted towards sinners who repented, the warmth, sympathy and understanding, and the sadness which he showed when others would not give him their friendship. That great human love of our Lord which he showed us by the way he acted, was his way of explaining to us, showing us, what the love of God should mean to you and me.

Never forget that the love of God for you is stronger, warmer, closer than any human love that you could experience, or any human love you could have for another person; it's that warm, that strong, that close.

Many of us grow up with the idea that God is a kind of judge looking at us to see if we do right or wrong, and we can grow up with fear – be too frightened. Of course God is judge and of course we should have the right kind of fear, but the fear of not wanting to displease somebody we love – not the fear of receiving punishment from one who is harsh.

❦

Prayer

Lord, through the example of your love and friendship, help me to come close to the loving Father.

Meeting God in prayer
Tuesday of the fifth week of Lent

❧

Scripture Reading

My soul thirsts for God, the God of life;
When shall I go to see the face of God?

Psalm 42:2

The philosopher, scientist and artist within us combine to lead us on throughout life on a journey of exploration, understanding and celebration of the whole of reality. It is my profound conviction that creation is a single and continuing expression of God's overwhelming goodness and love, even though there is much to bewilder and baffle, much left unexplained.

All discovery and research are, however, an exploration into the mind of God. All knowledge is a sharing in it. But at the end of our journey and striving, when we come into the presence of the living God, every other experience, all other beauty, will seem but straw. Then we shall know as we are known, love as we are loved, and God will be all in all. Restless minds will search no more when in the presence of absolute truth.

Be silent and still, and look also inwards, first at the darkness within, at conflicting emotions, at the emptiness of the heart, at inner wounds. We are in need of healing, or nearly always so, and in need too of being saved from what is base and ignoble. Whence come those lustful thoughts, involuntary angers, shameful jealousies. We are not as we should be.

When silent and still we can hear his voice speaking to us through our weakness and inadequacy, coaxing our minds to look for one who will bring order into that inner chaos, but most of all to give forgiveness and encouragement. He speaks, too, through anguish and agony, to draw us away from what separates from him to turn to him for serenity and inner peace.

※

Prayer

Father, help me to seek you in silence and stillness, to hear you showing me the way to peace.

Accepting the cross
Wednesday of the fifth week of Lent

❦

Scripture Reading

'Blessed be the God of Shadrach, Meshach and Abednego: he has sent his angel to rescue his servants who, putting their trust in him, defied the order of the king, and preferred to forfeit their own bodies rather than serve or worship any god but their own.'

Daniel 3:28

God allows us to be buffeted day by day by events and people. There are frustrations, misunderstandings, or we can just feel the effects of over-work and tiredness. Perhaps the trials of faith can be most burdensome of all. Sometimes it just seems that God is very remote and that can be a very great burden.

We learn as life goes on to adjust to many of these situations. We learn to take for ourselves the advice which we know we would give to others. We learn to cope with our problems and become less vulnerable to the pinpricks of daily living. We should, however, go further than this, and see in all moments of suffering moments of growth and advance in our hidden life with Christ.

We come to recognise the time of trial as a golden moment, and we can come to delight in these humiliations, the insults and hardships, the persecutions, the times of difficulty we undergo for God. We should practice when the moments of trial come, the art of accepting wholeheartedly and sincerely, the cross which God has lain upon our shoulders.

What peace there is to be gained by thanking God for allowing us to undergo the trial. That is not only good spiritual doctrine; it is also good common sense.

※

Prayer

Lord, help us to place our trust and faith in you. Use our suffering to strengthen us and bring us close to you.

Growing in our desire to know God

Thursday of the fifth week of Lent

❧

Scripture Reading

'If I were to seek my own glory, that would be no glory at all; my glory is conferred by the Father. I know him, and if I were to say: I do not know him, I should be a liar. But I do know him, and I faithfully keep his word.'

John 8:54–55

In our search for God we are trying to discover what he is like. Not the wisdom and science of this world, but something else which will be given to those who are humble, those who have learned from him who is gentle and lowly of heart, who not only learn something of him, but find rest in our souls. Surely that is what we are engaged in now, as we, through our prayer and reflection become silent and still, and listen.

The test of prayer life, spiritual life is, I believe, how we grow in our desire to see, know and to love him. So it is, or can be, when we reflect on his word, that word which was spoken to us, that word which is contemporary in every age. That word which is personal. Of course we can be overcome by doubts, of course in serious life of prayer there will be periods of darkness, of course there will be times when we have to struggle. We don't live in the light of friendship in our minds, or the warmth of friendship in our hearts. When we experience this it is a gift. But we have to constantly pray for the gift, be open to receive it, especially in Jesus Christ, the Word made flesh, and set out to explore what God is like.

❦

Prayer

Lord, through our prayer and reflection, help us to truly begin to know God.

An unconquered spirit
Friday of the fifth week of Lent

Scripture Reading

Do not gloat over me, my enemy: though I have fallen, I shall rise, though I live in darkness, Yahweh is my light. I must suffer the anger of Yahweh, for I have sinned against him, until he takes up my cause and rights my wrongs.

Micah 7:8–9

There are many sadnesses with which so many people are afflicted. I think of those wounds inflicted on so many women, men and children, our fellow human beings. I think of their pains and agonies that will not go away. What wounds? Five, as there are five in the body of Christ. I think of all forms of violence, of hunger, of oppression and persecution, of poverty, of sickness of every kind.

The world suffers, indeed, men, women and children. But these people, and I mean all those sorely tried by the blows that inflicted those wounds, share and go on sharing in our Lord's Passion, as we ourselves do from time to time.

I believe that these persons, victims of the five afflictions to which I have referred, can and often do learn through the experience of the Passion of our Lord the real secret of his resurrection – an inner peace, an inner freedom and joy. I have seen the triumph of Christ in the faces of victims of man's folly.

Of course we must work to remove the causes of these wounds of hunger, violence, and the rest. It is the Lord's command that we should do so. But there are other truths and other values which must also be recalled. The wounds may hurt, but they do not damage the spirit. An unconquered spirit is Christ's triumph. Inner peace, inner joy, inner freedom, are his gifts.

❧

Prayer

Lord, bring your peace, joy and freedom to all, and especially to those who suffer from oppression of every kind.

Religion in the public sphere
Saturday of the fifth week of Lent

✻

Scripture Reading

'I shall make them into one nation in my own land, and one king is to be king of them all; they will no longer form two nations, nor be two separate kingdoms ... I will be their God, they shall be my people.'

Ezekiel 37:22, 27

There is not, and cannot be, a total separation between the sacred and the secular worlds, as if God might be found on one channel but never on the others. Shafts of the glory of God can touch us in any context, at any moment, allowing us to glimpse a deeper purpose and significance behind our everyday concerns.

The religious instinct belongs, I believe, to human nature as such, though it will find expression in different religious responses. Once that instinct is awakened, and we focus our minds and hearts on God, we may come to see more clearly what should be the right priorities in our lives and thus how better to serve him and one another. We come, too, to realise that we are all but stewards in the Lord's vineyard, answerable, not only to the electorate and the judgement of history, but above all to the judgement of God.

Now religion is indeed always personal, but it is never private. Religious commitment requires us to live and work in accordance with our faith. It will inevitably have a bearing on public life. What we treasure most in our hearts, whatever gives meaning and purpose to our lives is revealed by the way we relate to each other. This is, of course, true also even if we do not give that treasure a religious name. We are missionaries to each other for the values that are really important to each one of us.

Prayer

Father, help my love for you inform my work, my relationships with others, every aspect of my life and be a witness to you.

The triumph of Christ
Palm Sunday

❧

Scripture Reading

The crowds who went in front of him and those who followed were all shouting 'Hosanna to the Son of David! Blessings on him who comes in the name of the Lord! Hosanna in the highest heavens!' And when he entered Jerusalem, the whole city was in turmoil. 'Who is this?' people asked, and the crowds answered, 'This is the prophet Jesus from Nazareth in Galilee.'

Matthew 21:9–11

Our Lord entered into Jerusalem in triumph and then just a few days later he was humiliated, tortured and executed. The contrast between Palm Sunday's procession and the events of Good Friday is all too clear: triumph on one day, and total humiliation and disaster on the other.

Of course, it is Holy Saturday which provides the clue and gives the whole explanation of why we call this Holy Week. Because the triumph, the real triumph, came through the Passion and death of our Lord, and this because of the resurrection.

The story ends well, that is why we read it, why we meditate on it, why we celebrate. The story ends well because the resurrection is the triumph – sin and death will be overcome.

It is not always easy for all of us to spend Holy Week as a special week, thoughtfully and prayerfully. But as far as we can we should plan now to steal time out of a busy life, just to re-read the story of the Passion, and think about it in a prayerful and loving way.

※

Prayer

Lord, help me to spend time with you during this week, as we commemorate your Passion, your death, and your resurrection.

A just society
Monday of Holy Week

❧

Scripture Reading

I, Yahweh, have called you to serve the cause of
right; I have taken you by the hand and formed you;
I have appointed you as covenant of the people and
light of the nations, to open the eyes of the blind, to
free captives from prison, and those who live in
darkness from the dungeon.

Isaiah 42:6–7

The state and the individual citizen must look to
the cause of the evil that people suffer. The
resources of the whole Church, as well as those
of individual Christians, must be put at the service of the
poor. It is encouraging to find practical examples of
individual and social response to need at work among
people.

It is important for all of us that we give wherever and
whenever we come up against need. But we can't be
content simply to offer aid. We need to seek – and we do
seek, wherever possible – to reform the structures which

perpetrate injustice and inhibit development. We lose no opportunity to urge public authorities at every level to undertake their proper responsibility for the welfare of all, especially for the poor and disadvantaged. Furthermore, we are concerned with suffering both at home and abroad. We try to respond to distress while seeking, at the same time, lasting remedies in order to prevent further suffering.

Christians have their own understanding of the reasons for building a more just and equal society. The Old Testament – sacred to both Jew and Christian – teaches us that human beings are made in the image and likeness of God. When this truth is not acknowledged, or is denied in practice, then the weak, the needy and the disadvantaged are neglected. Men and women – whatever their colour or creed, whatever their material circumstances – reflect something of the beauty and the truth of God. Each one is precious in the sight of the loving Father. Each has a dignity and a destiny from God which can never be denied or ignored. We have to respect this inner worth and absolute value. It is, then, unthinkable that a Christian should regard the well-being of any individual as unimportant or irrelevant.

❧

Prayer

Father, help me to build a just society which recognises the dignity of every person, created in your precious image.

A space which only God can fill
Tuesday of Holy Week

Scripture Reading

Islands, listen to me, pay attention remotest peoples. Yahweh called me before I was born, from my mother's womb he pronounced my name. 'I will make you the light of the nations so that my salvation may reach to the ends of the earth.'

Isaiah 49:1, 6

We need to reach out to society but, more directly and immediately, to individuals. Despite the evidence of secularisation, it is absolutely clear that there remains in the heart of each individual a space which only God can fill. There is a religious instinct, a hunger for God, which is often not recognised and which seeks satisfaction in many eccentric ways. This provides us with a constant opportunity for direct evangelisation for dialogue about the things of God.

In an age of change and uncertainty, people ask profound questions, about life itself, about suffering, about death, about love and what makes life worthwhile. People seek assurance and light. They respond if they are presented with a unifying reality which is in every way good, true and beautiful. Today – as always – the heart of mankind and its longings reach out beyond the here and now, beyond our present world, in search of the infinite and the eternal.

Without question there is a yearning for unity among peoples, a rejection of whatever discriminates or marginalizes others. There is an instinct for justice and a longing for peace. There is a growing question for the physical wholeness of creation, for the exercise of adequate stewardship towards the finite resources of our planet.

The whole people of God can undertake here that task for unity, justice and peace which is an integral part of the Gospel.

❧

Prayer

Father, fill me with the desire to spread the unity, justice and peace of your Gospel throughout the whole world.

Our own betrayal of Christ
Wednesday of Holy Week

❧

Scripture Reading

He answered, 'Someone who has dipped his hand
into the dish with me, will betray me. The Son of
Man is going to his fate, as the scriptures say he will,
but alas for that man by whom the Son of Man is
betrayed!' Judas, who was to betray asked in his
turn, 'Not I, Rabbi, surely?'

Matthew 26:23–25

When I think of Judas, words begin to fail, for is
there anything more dastardly than betrayal –
can anything be lower than to treat another
human being in that manner?

There is sin in the world, and we are sinners. We are
right always to meditate at length and in depth on the
mercy of God and the love of God for us. Rich and
encouraging though this is, let us not be blinded to the
reality of sin which is part of our unhappy world, and it
is a foolish and dangerous thing to point the finger at
other people without taking note of our own sin.

There are of course those sins of weakness when we are overcome by passion, by our weaknesses. They are different from those calculated and deliberate decisions to do that which is wrong. But in some measure all of us are burdened with sin, and that thought should not escape us. Christ suffered and died because of sin: not just the sin of Judas, but the sin of the world, the sin of men and women down the ages. So each of us in some way contributed to his Passion and death.

That is not a reason for being depressed, or overcome with sorrow. There must be sorrow, of course, there must be avowal of our sin, an expression of our sorrow, and a putting right what has been done wrong. The times in which we live demand that we have a more vivid awareness of sin in the world. Whenever we harden our hearts to the needs of others, we sin. Whenever we pursue pleasure for its own sake, we sin.

There is a need for that awareness today, because for goodness to prevail effort is needed.

※

Prayer

Lord, we are all burdened by sin. Help us to acknowledge our sins, and to turn away from sin to you.

In silence with the Father
Maundy Thursday

❧

Scripture Reading

Jesus came to a small estate called Gethsemane;
and he said to his disciples, 'Stay here while I go
over there to pray'. He took Peter and the two sons
of Zebedee with him. And sadness came over him,
and great distress. Then he said to them, 'My soul is
sorrowful to the point of death. Wait here and keep
awake with me.'

Matthew 26:36–38

Silence is a good friend – and one that guides us to
find God to be with us. Our Lord left the supper
table and walked into the night to find silence – to
be alone – and in that silence to be with his Father. It
was not a peaceful silence, for he was in agony, blood and
sweat on his brow, as he struggled to accept the suffering
that he must undergo, and the failure of those closest to
him, who failed him when he needed them most. He
had gone to find silence and solitude to be with his
Father.

He told his disciples, Peter, James and John to watch and pray – to be with him, close by, and to be at prayer with him. They found it hard. They dropped off to sleep while he struggled within, praying first to be freed from his agony, then to accept to drink the chalice of pain. They slept, and later, under pressure, they left him altogether.

In prayer we may share with him our agonies and our struggles too, and not least the struggle to accept God's will when that seems hard to do. We may speak to him about the pains and sufferings of those whom we know and love, our relatives and friends, not forgetting strangers too.

Above all, he asks us to join him just for a bit tonight, alone, and in silence.

※

Prayer

Father, help me to find you in silence, to speak to you in silence, to silently accept your will.

The anguish of the Cross
Good Friday

❧

Scripture Reading

From the sixth hour there was darkness over all the land until the ninth hour. And about the ninth hour, Jesus cried out in a loud voice, 'Eli, eli, lama sabachthani?', that is, 'My God, my God, why have you deserted me?' ... Jesus, again crying out in a loud voice, yielded up his spirit.

Matthew 27:45, 46, 50

The words of Psalm 22 which our Lord prayed on the Cross expressed the experience of darkness and abandonment, the experience which was his at that moment.

We pray those words today to recall the anguish of mind which the Son of God knew; recall too the anguish of mind and sense of abandonment and darkness experienced by men and women down the ages, and no less in our own time.

There are many who experience darkness and abandonment. Our prayer is that they, and indeed perhaps we also, should find in that experience the light which dispels the darkness, and sense the oneness with God which empties abandonment of its anguish, and that we should find life, life hidden with Christ in God which is the Easter grace and fruit of that redemption about which we think and pray, and sense so poignantly today.

※

Prayer

Lord, help me to find light in the darkness, oneness with you when I feel abandoned, the life in you which you won for us.

The light of the Spirit
Holy Saturday

🌿

Scripture Reading

The night is over and the real light is already shining. Anyone who claims to be in the light but hates his brother is still in the dark. But anyone who loves his brother is living in the light and need not be afraid of stumbling.

I John 2:8b–10

There is today stillness, silence, almost a sense of emptiness. It is a time of waiting; of expectation; of preparation for the great celebration tonight; and as today progresses and the sun goes down, we start our celebration in darkness.

Sometimes I think that the darkness which descends matches in some manner the darkness in the minds of many of us. Just as at the moment when light shines again we see familiar surroundings once more, perhaps after darkness we tend to see things differently, in a new light.

It is a festival of light tonight and there is one light

above all for which we must pray, and that is the light of the Holy Spirit. When light is present, there is recognition of what is there. So it is when the Holy Spirit touches our minds, there is light and recognition of what is there.

So as preparation, on this day of waiting and expecting, let us pray that our minds may be given that light to recognise in him who died and rose again from the dead, our true Saviour, Jesus Christ.

❧

Prayer

Father, may the Spirit you sent to open minds dispel the darkness in my heart, and fill me with the light of new life.

The good news of salvation: he is risen!

Easter Sunday

❧

Scripture Reading

It was very early on the first day of the week and still dark, when Mary of Magdala came to the tomb. She saw that the stone had been moved away from the tomb and came running to Simon Peter and the other disciple. 'They have taken the Lord out of the tomb' she said 'and we do not know where they have put him.' So Peter set out with the other disciple to go to the tomb ... he saw and he believed. Till this moment they had failed to understand the teaching of scripture, that he must rise from the dead.

John 20:1–9

Christ is risen!
Easter challenges us each year. Do we believe that Christ truly rose from the dead? Belief in Christ's Resurrection is fundamental and essential to being a Christian.

Christianity makes demands. It is not an easy option. Its founder, Jesus Christ, called for a change of heart, a turning to God. He demanded a change in ways of thinking and in behaviour. That call is still being made to us in our day. Shall we listen to it?

The tomb was empty. Everyone at the time agreed on that, but the Apostles had been slow to understand what had happened. Once Peter and John had verified the fact for themselves, they understood the teaching of the scriptures, that he must rise from the dead. So later on, Peter, addressing Cornelius' household, told them that they were witnesses to the resurrection of the Lord, and they had to proclaim the good news.

We have the same duty to give witness to the fact that Christ is risen from the dead. Death has lost its hold over mankind. Death is not, for us, the end of the story. It is the beginning of a new chapter. There is life after death; it is life with God. Our present life is to prepare for that.

❦

Prayer

Lord, your rising opens the door to eternal life for us. Help us to prepare for our lives with you, to spread the good news of your resurrection throughout the whole world.